SHE; THE CHAOS

Fiercely feeling the life, she lives

Ipsita

BookLeaf
Publishing

India | USA | UK

Made with ❤ on the BookLeaf Publishing Platform
www.bookleafpub.in
www.bookleafpub.com

Dedication

To the beautiful souls I've met over the last 28 years, who have inspired me, directly or indirectly, to write my heart onto a blank canvas.

And most importantly, to the little girl within, who always loved herself deeply and stood strong through it all.

Preface

"We write, because sometimes words breathe better than we can."

Drafting this takes me back to a brief memory, showing my first poem, about two decades ago, to my dearest mother. She appreciated it as if it were the most wonderful creation she had ever witnessed, inspiring me to write my heart down in an unapologetic way.

Then life happened. The little girl grew; with time, experiences, and acquaintances, her pen becoming a silent confidante, capturing and releasing many moments and memories. Penning down emotions became a constant source of solace, leading to the habit of scribbling heartfelt feelings on blank pages and spaces.

These compiled creations mostly reflect the emotional roller coaster of my late twenties sweet-sour affairs of self-love, the search for validation, and the overwhelming emotions of longing and questioning.

I hope these poems offer you comfort, solace, and that sweet ache of recognition in shared longings and unanswered questions, just as they did for me while writing. Thank you for joining me in these spaces.

Acknowledgements

It takes an artist to truly appreciate art. I'm blessed to have such beautiful souls on this journey, in the form of family, friends, and acquaintances.

Though it took a while for me to openly share my writings in various forms of expression, I will forever remain indebted to every soul who believed in the tender, aspiring heart of this "forever little girl," who fiercely embraced every emotion life presented.

Your belief has given these words a voice.

Undefined, Yet Real

Echoes of Questions,
Room vacuumed by those blank answers;

The shadowed shadows,
through those Semitransparent window curtains;

The ink demanded to flow,
On that undefined path
Lead by Pauses, Phases
& Unnotified staycations!!
Strange?

No. Reality: She answers!

Ink, Steam, and Silence

The pleasure of reading those lines,
While sipping that custom-made coffee.
She was assured;

Happiness, shaped by the vague words of creation,
Or the briefest of emotions.

Beyond everything,
She longed for that tethering spark of excitement,
Trying to picture her heart smiling !

The Lean into Dawn

3

Sweet pain of feeling over-felt,
Like the stormy night heading towards the dawn.

Shouldered sighs turning into watery drops,
Stumbled bumps shaping into a fine road ;

On the Verge

4

Like an old tree standing still,
A brimming pot on the verge of overflow,
A long sentence aching for a pause.

A river tracing its course,
Wondering where the estuary opens.

Unheard Echoes

5

The blanket beneath
The blank space;
A pause between the chaos :

Echoes of silence tornadoing the paths;
Return to that unidirectional Chaos.

Told in Touch

The beauty of holding hands
The fingers across each other ;

Fitting into those little gaps
Each stroke depicting the story of lingered moments,
Caressing the skin in contact
Showered the love, care and belongingness ;

Slendering slowly into each other
Walking down the crowded streets to walking across

Every hand held story
Wove the beauty in time ;

Of Light and Loss

The cloud drive
Roads led by fairy lights,

With billions of blind curves
Petals of those blossomed trees
Shedding the skin throughout

Had theren't been any bumps on the way
Had the brakes been a bit smoother.

A Pause That Moves

The arm rest of the chairs
On those crowded terminals !

Hah ! What not they have witnessed;

From tears of sparkling joys
To the moments of unbothered solace ;
With moments questioned with zero expectations to be answered,
To a handful of surprises turning into Exclamations!

The journey, the pauses
And everything in between!!

Alas!
That itself is "IT";

Unfolded Letters

Fairy tales
Defined by those Bollywood movies,
Romantic novels, and the tales of her dreams.

Remained there,
Like that water droplet wishing to fall,
Yet standing tall against gravity.

The gurgling of an empty stomach,
And the woven sores of a trembling heart,
Needed assurance, still bravely folded.
Added pointers yet remained fully blank.

To the aged pages
and
bundles of unfiltered letters,
She wrote to her
For her fairytale.

Shelter of Arms

Beyond a boundary,
Beyond the alphabets,
Spilling in silence, yet saying it all ;

Squinching oneself down,
Fitting into those arms just right,
Resting the head on their chest,
Or sinking into the curve of their shoulder back ;
To collect all the moments of warmth
Without loosing a nanosecond down;

How beautiful,
The human touch;
Hugging the heart out,
Holding without needing to ask;

No exchange of words,
No exchange of thoughts,
Just emotions,
Doing what they do;

A pause of the halt,
A halt of the pause !

The Fulfilling Unknown

From a space
Just behind the rib bones
Located in a small corner
With flow of chills flowing throughout

Or just a under mixed layer
Flowing through every blood vein

A soothing full filing question mark !!

The Solitary Strength

12

Prohibited, restricted, forcedly closed doors,
Pushing through, against the wind,
While trudging down the road,
She held her own, choking the unwanted aside.

She held her tight,
Held her amidst all the storms.

For at the end of the night,

She, Her, and Herself;

Like always!

Whys of Whys'

The Whys of the ages
The why of the existence

The "Whys" of the Whys' ;

Do all of these make sense
Or just mere co-existence with the pseudo surfacing!!

Again, boils down to another "Why".

Unexplored Strings

The unsaid strings
The never known bonds,

The unestimated distances
The unbeatable emotions

Ending up
Taking up the shape of few letters
Inked on the blanks
With the inks from an unknown pot ;

Blank Overwhelmed

The shared hope
In that closed room ;
Putting the pen aside & page blank

Infinite words flew across
Yet blank ;
For them to witness;
And quite overwhelming for those
Who it's meant to be !!

Realized once again;
How strange
The relationship between
Her pen
&
Any blank page is!!

Blank Ceiling of Worth

The worth and worthiness collide,
As she gazes at the white ceiling wide,
The ticking clock whispers in the air,
A past conversation lingers there.

A talk of joy, of life's embrace,
Lost in the frantic, hurried race.
The daily grind, the chase for bread,
Anxious steps, where fears are fed.

No time to speak to those who care,
Yet digital pings fill the empty air.
Is this called living, or just a game!
A rat race, chasing fleeting fame.

Chasing gratification, swift and bright,
While leaving love behind, out of sight.
For whom she matters, she drifts away,
A stranger to Herself each day.

The Compass of Ink

The tip started thinking
Which was very rare for her :
There was a clash between the paper and the pages
afterwards

She was there,
Yet NOT !

The questions; exclamations
Did they make sense

Why! Why was and always been the question

Lately realized ;
The inks have been flowing in the same direction!!

Is it leading somewhere?

Or she refuses to acknowledge?!

Before the Map

Beginning

The starting point of that unseen road
The unlimited questions of those million possibilities

Is it the distance between the question and answer
Or the fear associated with that question

Road, estuary or mirage
Everything, is beyond that point

Life, road, blessings
Of that curvaceous road ;

The Hush Too Brief

Gulped out like the discarded Junk
Not letting silence echo too long
Dropped that heavy loathsome load
On a surface already overwhelmed

Still, the weight will linger
Until the droplet meets that gentle touch

Calmest Pause

The Hold of Night
The body misses
The calmest pause.

While leaving everything behind,
She hugged you and was there for the whole moment.
Rested her head on the chest,
While closing you tight.
The spark is young and fresh,
Like that unattended wound
Needing dosage of cures.

Do you feel the same?

Or just me,
Voking out blabbered thoughts,
While feeling it skin by skin.

Are u there?
Will u be there?
Should I be there?

Beyond Definition

The nights of unified rhythms, undefined shadows

Sorrows, Bliss & the in between

Ever-changing letters with that constant backdrop

Why; Why Not ?
Until When

Yet "Define that" Not !

Wish it was dug to the depth:
To which the nights can't reach
Nor the sunrays of hopes, wishes or promises;

Memoirs Without Markers

Had there been no dates
Would you have ever
bothered to capture
"Me," "Us,"
and Memoirs of Us?

If no clocks were ticking:
Would your heart ever known fullness ;
not by counting hours,
rather letting tenderness swell to its peak !

Hadn't there been a calendar,
How
You / Me
would have grieved
about the griefs!

Fragmented Mirror

Wandered. Puzzled.

Breath after breath
with a longer pause,
a shorter depth;

Loud voices
silent enough to
be clarified.

Heavy to the core,
questionable from
questions;

Have enough; yet not.
Have soul?
Aimless enough.

Subtle Calm

It was the mindy breeze,
The calming whispers
& the talcumy touches
She was eyeing for;

The echoed voice
In that silence
She enjoyed;

The calming pause
In that silent blink
She embraced;

The unspoken emotions
Reserved for herself
Was just firmed :

Her Becoming

A mystery she was unaware of
A mystery she has started loving;

Starting from her coffee dark & strong
To the vulnerability she has been carrying throughout;

Have the definitions been defined yet
Has the page been filled yet with all those questions;

If I say, that's how she has been gathering her Solace
If she says so !!

Space:Home:Walls

A Home, some space
She can call "Home"

Space of warmth, love
Might be devoid of walls
Space of tranquility
Where putting on layers of clothes is not required;

Corners of flowers
Corners of old books
Shelf designated for handwritten letters
A wall of purple & brown;
Self insulated doors & windows
With tiny holes for those
Fireflies to blink in

The curtains as she desires
Or so, the space becomes
The "HOME"
Let's say the person to be keen ;

The Geometry

Breaking the broken
Hurts the fist
Said the reflection in those broken triangles;

Punctuated Silences

An ache
the ache of constant inconstancy,
born of a served notion of existence,
tethered to worldly disparities.

An era with no synonyms
for its attended imparities.

With zillions of punctuations
To an unminded, aching heart.

Almost Mutual

You said, "It feels like you."
You said, "I like it, because it feels like you."

Then my heart aches and questions:
How could you let me go, when you know
I like you enough
to like me liking you?

One Last Time

Can we meet one last time
Resume looking into the eyes,
Like that moment just before a kiss;

Can I rest my head on your chest,
Feel your heartbeat match the ache in mine,
For the one last time!

Can I let myself,
Allow me to allow you
To look at me,
With that calm, serene tenderness
You always wore for me;

Just that breath,
that closeness,
One last time.